Sell Your House ...
Successfully

Don't Hire A Realtor® Until You Read This Book

Teri Connors
Licensed Associate Broker
Award Winning Author

Sell Your House...Successfully
www.SellYourHouseBook.com

Publisher
10-10-10 Publishing
Markham, ON
Canada

Printed in Canada and the United States of America

TABLE OF CONTENTS

DEDICATION

This book is dedicated to all the homeowners that need to sell their home, or have sold a home and had a bad experience, and need guidance.

ACKNOWLEDGEMENTS

Deciding to write a book is easy; the trying part is being dedicated. Many, many people have given me encouragement along the way and I would like to sincerely thank them, starting with three very important men in my life—my three loves.

First, my two amazing sons, Craig and Steven. I couldn't ask for better sons; you both have given me so much joy, more than you will ever know. I am so proud of you both. Craig and Steven, you make me want to be a better person.

Second, I would like to thank my partner, Al. I am so grateful I get to spend my life with you. Without your constant encouragement, I don't think this book would have come to fruition.

Thank you to my friends who knew about the book, for your encouragement and positive attitude, and for believing in me. Thank you for always asking "How's the book coming along?" Love to Darlene, Owen, Elly, Barbara, Debra, Jinny, Billie, Mary, Karl, Denice and Tina.

Thank you to my cousins Marilyn and Judy for giving me ideas and sharing your knowledge about writing. We may not see each other as often as we would like; however, we know we're only a phone call away. Love you.

I wouldn't be where I am today without the help of broker/owner, Michael J. Morris, manager, Ted Gounelas, admins, Laraine and Liz, and the awesome fellow agents at Coldwell Banker M&D Good Life.

I would like to thank my friend and mentor, Raymond Aaron. I had no idea when I met Raymond that he would change my life so dramatically. Raymond has taught me the power of a positive attitude and has given me the confidence to pursue my dream of helping homeowners sell their home successfully.

I would like to acknowledge Rosa Greco, my book architect. Rosa kept me going and guided me step by step. I'm sure I was one of her more challenging clients; however, her persistence and patience paid off.

Thank you to all my wonderful clients. I truly appreciate your trust in me to help guide you through the journey of selling or buying a home. It was a pleasure working with all of you.

Last, but certainly not least, I would like to thank the reader of this book. You are the reason an idea became a book. You are behind the hours and hours of writing, editing, and making sure that every detail is correct and, finally, getting this book published. I hope you learn many, many aspects from this book; however, if it's just one new idea, I have done my job. Thank you for being my inspiration.

TESTIMONIALS

12/29/2016 – kearneyjr14
Bought a home in 2016 in Rocky Point, NY 11778.
She really made our home buying experience easy. Always responsive and upfront. Focused on our needs. Really is a wonderful caring person, and I would be happy to recommend her to anyone.

12/27/2016 – TLPT
Bought a Condo home in 2016 for approximately $200K in Middle Island, NY.
I am writing to highlight Teri Connors' exceptional service and compassion throughout our first property buying experience. From the start, Teri was personable, kind, knowledgeable, and genuine. Teri made sure to let us know what steps to proactively take in order to smoothly transition through each phase of the buying process. We closed on our new place less than a week ago and couldn't be happier. Thank you Teri, you're the best!

04/06/2016 – mmile2

Sold a Single Family home in 2015 for approximately $275K in Patchogue, NY.

Teri is such an honest and caring real estate agent. She gave us advice on the best way to present our home and was available for all our questions and needs. She worked extremely hard to get our home sold quickly and for a fair price that we could live with. Now, six months after we sold our home and moved out of state, we still get phone calls from Teri asking how we are doing. She is truly one real estate agent that we would recommend, and we are now proud to call her our dear friend as well.

04/05/2016 – joegoo

Sold a Single Family home in 2015 for approximately $150K in Patchogue, NY.

Teri is an extremely hard working agent. She handled every detail during the showing, offer, and closing process. We were totally satisfied and will use her again when needed.

2/04/2016 – user63233119

Sold a Condo home in 2013 in Port Jefferson, NY.

Teri sold my townhouse in Pt. Jefferson in 2013 – she was amazing, reliable, always available, and on top of everything! Definitely could not have done it without her. Due to my work schedule, I was never available to be home to let potential buyers or Teri in; I trusted her with full access to my house and never had a worry. Highly recommended!

ABOUT THE AUTHOR

Teri Connors, Associate Broker, GRI, CBR, e-PRO is a Realtor® on Long Island, New York. She retired from a telecommunications company, after working there for over 33 years, to pursue her lifelong passion of real estate. "One of the reasons I got into real estate was because I had such a bad experience with the agents and the process in selling and buying my homes. I want buyers and sellers to have a positive, stress-free experience. It's also one of the reasons for writing this book." In her spare time, Teri enjoys spending time with her sons, family, friends, and ballroom dancing with her fiancé. Teri is heavily involved with Toastmasters, where she is Secretary for her home club and VP of Membership for her second club. In her day to day life, she works on having a positive attitude and leading a well-balanced, harmonious lifestyle. Teri works with mentors and learns everything she can to create a better life for herself and everyone around her.

FOREWORD

Selling a home can be either a stressful situation or an enjoyable one, and I highly suggest the later. You may think that all you need to do to sell your home is set your price, and then wait for a buyer to come along and take it off your hands. As a homeowner who has sold and purchased several homes, I can tell you that there are many things you can do to make the transaction easier. Teri points out many things you can take advantage of to help make your sale a successful one.

From the start, Teri enlightens you to the many advantages of selecting the proper Realtor® to assist you. I can personally attest to the many benefits that come from selecting the proper agent. Another thing she reminds you of is that choosing the selling price is not simply deciding how much money you want for your home. Teri tells you about factors that can impact how much traffic you get, and how to select the best buyer for your home, which is not necessarily the one with the highest offer. Some other important points to consider are how to market your home, and how to maximize exposure and make it visible to the greatest number of qualified buyers as possible.

These are just a few of the considerations you need to address when selling your home; there are many, many more. This book will shed light on those things. Whether you are a repeat seller or a first-time seller, there is information here for you! Read about the entire process before you put your home on the market, so you know what to expect and are better prepared in any type of market. Even if you are an experienced seller, you can find something new here; something you didn't fully understand before or a new idea you hadn't thought about. I know I did.

Raymond Aaron
New York Times Bestselling Author
Real Estate Investor

CHAPTER 1
WHEN IS THE BEST TIME TO SELL MY HOME?

The dream of homeownership has grown over the past 2 years, according to the MacArthur Foundation. In 2014, 50% of the population believed real estate was an excellent long-term investment. In 2015, there was 56% of Americans believing real estate is a great way to build wealth, and that number rose up to 60%, in 2016. If you are considering selling a home, and you probably are since you're reading this book, you have picked a great time to sell.

I'm sure you have heard or thought the best time to put your house on the market is in the spring. Although this might be right for some, it may not be best for you.

Maybe it's because the flowers are in full bloom. Or because families can be in their new residence before school starts. Maybe it's because it's just what everyone does.

The spring is the most popular time to sell a house because of the facts stated above. Unfortunately, many homeowners think that is the ONLY time to sell their house and, if they decide they want or need to sell in the fall or winter, will often wait until that perceived best time, which is the following spring.

On the flip side, I'm sure you have heard winter is the worst time to sell; at least, that is what you hear from people. Several reasons might be that buyers aren't out looking for homes in the cold months, there is too much snow, the house doesn't have the attractive curb appeal like it does in the spring or summer months, it gets dark earlier in the day and buyers like to look at homes in the daylight, the list goes on and on.

The simple reality of it all is, whenever you need or want to sell, it is the right time. When a buyer is looking to purchase a home, it doesn't matter if there is snow on the ground, or the flowers are in bloom and the grass is green; they need to buy a house—that's the bottom line. You may miss out on the perfect buyer if you wait for the perceived *perfect time* to sell your house.

One of my clients sold their home in late summer and transferred to a cold climate area. The family planned on renting a home so they could enjoy looking for a home without the pressure of having to find the perfect home while moving cross country. The time of year they will look for their new home will be fall or winter, depending on how long it takes them to find the perfect home. Not all buyers can wait until the spring. They need to buy a house now—your house—and, by waiting, you will miss the opportunity of having that perfect buyer purchase your home. Like my clients, you may want to sell your home and rent a temporary place so you can enjoy the buying process without the pressure of juggling 2 closings simultaneously. The most meticulously planned sale can run into unforeseen delays and obstacles. Having your home already sold will also make you more appealing when purchasing your next home; an unencumbered buyer is exponentially more appealing than one that still needs to sell their home.

Many times, homeowners have resided in a home for many decades, raising their wonderful families and enjoying many, many, happy times, but now the children are all grown, with children of their own, with their own lives, and the house that was once perfect is now too large. There is too much maintenance to keep up, the taxes are too high, and you're paying taxes for schools which your family is no longer utilizing. Not to mention the energy bills such as electric, water, and heat. It is obvious the time has come to allow another owner to enjoy everything the home has to offer. That next homeowner may very well be a family that is outgrowing their current home, and needs more bedrooms, more bathrooms, or a larger yard.

You know you have outgrown your current home if...

Your home is your castle—your own little piece of the American dream—but lately, your little corner of the world has been feeling cramped, and you find yourself eyeing those larger homes. It may be time to pull up stakes and move on from your starter home.

Growing Family

If you've added to your family in recent years, you may have more bodies than bedrooms. That two-bedroom, 1-bath home may have been the perfect home when it was just you and your spouse; but with two kids, you're starting to have turf wars over the play area.

Overflowing with Stuff

From an overflowing toy chest to closets packed so tightly with shoes and coats that you risk an avalanche every time you open the door, your home just doesn't have the space to hold all your things. You may even have needed to move some things off-site, spending money to rent storage space to keep that antique dresser your grandmother left you, or the set of state spoons you carefully collected during your college years.

Your Kitchen is Outdated

How convenient is your kitchen? Does it work efficiently? Can you store all your pots and pans? Can you get to the item in the back of the cabinet without emptying the whole cabinet? Is it too small to entertain your family and friends?

No Rest for the Weary

You'd love to spend an afternoon soaking in the tub, but before the warmth of the water can take you away, there's a banging on the door of the only bathroom in the house, and a chorus of "hurry up" invading your quiet time. What about that *man cave* you dreamed of? Those visions of a big screen television were shattered by the realization that you needed somewhere for the kids to sleep.

No Room for Extras

When you first moved in, the two-car garage doubled as your woodworking shop. Now, the equipment has been sent to storage to make room for the family's second car. You'd love to take up organic gardening, but your tiny yard barely has room for a grill and a lawn chair. You'd love to host your friends visiting from out of state, but there is hardly room for their luggage, much less them.

Changes in Career

You may have opted for a starter home when you first entered the market because you had a smaller income. The good news is that now, thanks to changes in careers or promotions at work, and all the equity you have accumulated in your home, you can afford to move to a home with greater square footage and room for your growing family, which will provide the space needed for many years, and lots and lots of happy memories.

Home prices across the country are rising at a rapid pace! Contact your local real estate agent today and take advantage of the opportunity to now give your family the most space at the best price.

Buyers don't care what time of year it is; they just know the home they're in doesn't fit their needs any longer, and they need it NOW!

So, as you can see, there are many reasons for selling a home, just like there are many reasons to purchase a home. The time of year or season becomes secondary to the need to move.

Yes, in the springtime, the grass is greener, the flowers are in bloom, the weather is warmer, and there will be more houses for sale, increasing the amount of competition, which will give the buyers an upper hand due to an abundance of inventory. Also, in the winter months, the buyers are much more serious about purchasing a home. Any time a buyer bundles up in their winter coat, gloves, hat, scarf, and snow boots, they're not going shopping at the mall—they're serious about finding and buying that perfect home.

The market is active all year long; if you need to sell, then sell. If you wait for the perfect time, you just might wait yourself right out of the market.

We will discuss how to price your home and make it appealing to buyers, in another chapter.

A word to the wise, don't wait so long that the interest rates go up, thereby reducing the purchasing power of the buyer. This is something that has a huge impact on the sale of your home, and it's something smart homeowners are aware of. However, for some reason, the average homeowners decide not to take this into account when selling their home. Maybe, as Realtor's®, we're not communicating what a huge impact this has on the sale of your home.

If you would like current mortgage rates and data on a buyer's purchasing power, and oodles of additional helpful information, visit:

Sellyourhousebook.com

CHAPTER 2
GETTING THE MOST MONEY FROM THE SALE OF YOUR HOME

Getting the biggest bang for your money isn't as difficult as you might think. Chances are, your competition isn't aware of these awesome but almost effortless steps, or doesn't care. In this chapter, you will find the easiest, cheapest, and quickest way to add value to your home, with little effort on your part. I will discuss what to change about your home that will put it in a positive light in the buyer's eyes and will have your house standing head and shoulders above your competition. The best way to go about adding value to your home is to clean, declutter, add or enhance curb appeal, remove all odors, paint, and keep up on maintenance. Treat your home as a product the minute it goes on the market; it is no longer your home. What you like in your home doesn't matter; it's all about what potential buyers like, and then getting them to buy.

Cleaning

Cleaning is by far the easiest, quickest, and cheapest way to get more bang for your buck, and put more money in your pocket. However, for some reason, this basic, easy to do tip is the most overlooked.

Let's start with the cleaning of your home. We all clean the bathrooms, kitchen, floors, etc., usually on a weekly basis, and sometimes on a daily basis, but what about the ceiling fans, under the couches, or behind the furniture? Don't forget the cobwebs on the ceilings and light fixtures. Clean the appliances: the stove and oven, microwave, refrigerator, and the dishwasher. The dishwasher? Yes, I said dishwasher. Have you ever noticed how it can get very grubby on the inside of the door and on the sides? All you need to do is give it a quick sponge. Imagine going to a very nice hotel. You've saved for a long time for this vacation—skipping lunches, eating out less, watching every penny for this exact moment. Let's say this beautiful hotel is in New York City, where a decent hotel can run you several hundred dollars for just one night. You open up the fridge or microwave, and EIKKK—dirt, crud, and even worse, hair! Now, imagine you're thinking of possibly purchasing a home with your hard-earned money: the money you scrimped and saved; the money you didn't spend going to the movies or eating out as much. You're excited but cautious about spending this money on a home; after all, it is one of the biggest decisions you will ever make. You liked the home online, told your agent about it, made an appointment to see it, and are now hoping it looks as good in person as it did in the pictures online. This might be the one you're seriously thinking about buying, and then, WHAM! You open the refrigerator and find hair. Is that cat hair? Human hair? And what was that? A cucumber? A pepper? Ewe, gross! What else is going on in this house? If they can't clean the fridge, what else are they neglecting? NO THANKS! It's on to the next house. You just lost a buyer, and all it would have taken was a little time to clean the mess and get rid of whatever the heck that was in the back of your refrigerator.

If you don't have the time to clean the house yourself, hire a professional cleaning company. The return on the investment of cleaning your home can have a huge impact on the impression buyers feel. All else being equal, cleaning your home is the easiest, least expensive thing you can do to make it more desirable.

Cleaning is an excellent way to make your home more appealing to buyers, but why stop there when there are other ways to enhance your home's desirability? Read on for other ways to help make your home a buyer's dream home.

Declutter

This is so easy; it's a no brainer! To declutter or not to declutter: this is the question. Of course, you should declutter. Take a good look at your house with new eyes. Have a friend or family member go through the house with you and point out where you can declutter. Closets are a great starting place. Start with the coat closet. You're moving anyway, so you may as well start donating those coats you no longer wear, that don't fit or are out of style. Take everything out of the closet and only put back what you absolutely need. If you're selling your home during the warm season, then pack up most of the coats. One time, I was showing a home to buyers and, when I opened the coat closet, a sea of blankets, toys, and other items came falling out onto the floor. Uh oh, no storage space in this home.

Next, go to the bedroom closets; take out everything you haven't worn in the past 2 years. Again, either donate or throw it away. If it's something sentimental, then pack it away—you're moving anyway. Only put back the items you absolutely need. Hang the remaining clothes by either season or color; just be sure the closet looks organized and uncluttered. The same goes for shoes, sneakers, and boots. The same also goes for linen closets, where you can take a small closet and make it appear larger. Fold the towels and sheets neatly. You can fold your bedsheets and then store them in the pillow cases so everything stays together neatly. Storage bins are great for all those odd shaped items; be sure to get a couple of different sizes. And, before putting anything in a bin, make sure it hasn't expired, or you no longer need it—why bother moving things if you're never going to use them again? For large, bulky blankets, consider using a vacuum seal bag; they work well, and the blankets won't take up so much space.

Don't forget the kitchen cabinets. Go through food items, making sure the items haven't expired; if they have, throw them out. Now that the kitchen cabinets are decluttered, make sure the doors all work, and the drawers open and close easily. Otherwise, buyers will want to discount the cost of new cabinets.

Pack up anything you won't be using in the next 6 months, or haven't used in the past year. You're moving anyway, and this will give you a great head start, while making the home appear larger and roomier. Just be sure to label the boxes really well to help you find things you need after the move to your new home. Don't forget the basement. Buyers want to be able to see the whole basement they're buying, not just look at it from the staircase and not be able to step in it and walk around. They'll want to see the electrical panel, alarm system, sprinkler system, oil tank and burner, so make sure they're not blocked. Sweep and dust the basement; nothing will chase the buyers out of your home faster than getting covered in cob webs. Make sure there is sufficient lighting to see the entire basement. If only one out of three bulbs work, the buyers may think there are electrical issues in the home. The same goes for the entire house—make sure it's cob web free and that every room has working lights. Clean up the garage. There's nothing like going to see a home with a 2-car garage, and the buyers can't even put a golf club in it.

Remember, whenever things are on top of cabinets or fall out of closets, or you can't walk through the basement or garage, it SCREAMS to buyers that there's no space in this home. If all of this cleaning out and decluttering seems too overwhelming, then set aside 15–30 minutes a day, put on some music that gets you moving, and work on one area at a time. Before you know it, in a week, you'll have so much more space and a head start on your packing—after all, you're moving anyway.

Buyers are now loving your home. They can picture themselves living there, and they want to make it their new home. All this is great but, wait; can we get them to fall in love with your home *before* they walk in the front door? Sure, we can, by applying the important ideas that are in the next section. Ignore these points, and it may be *bye, bye,* and onto the next home.

Curb Appeal

Buyers decide if they like your home in less than 30 seconds. Read that again: *in less than 30 seconds.* And if we can't get them in the door, then call it a day. One of the most important photographs of your home is the exterior, because it's usually the very first photo that buyers will see online or in a brochure. Think about when you're looking to purchase something or are deciding which restaurant to go to for dinner; you look for a reason NOT to purchase or dine at that restaurant. Today, over 93% of buyers begin their search online; it takes them seconds to either want to see more or, worse yet, go on to the next home, so curb appeal has to be at the top or your list.

Your home may have beautiful bathrooms and a modern, inviting kitchen, but the buyers have to get in the home to see and appreciate them. Look at your home from across the street. Take a good look at the roof, chimney, siding, windows, shutters, landscaping, front door, door bell, door hardware, walkway, driveway and apron, mailbox ... everything. Take stock of how it would look to a stranger, or someone who has never been to your home. Does it say, "Welcome, come in and relax," or "Ouch, I need help; please buy me?" Or, does it says something in between? Does the roof need to be repaired, or do you need a new roof? Mortgage companies will usually insist on a dry house; if the roof is in disrepair, don't wait until your buyer's mortgage company insists on it—get it done now. How are the gutters? I once showed a home where the sellers were asking a pretty penny for it, and there was a tree growing in the gutter! We couldn't miss it; it was right above the garage on the front of the house. So, clean the gutters, and you won't scare away buyers. How are the windows? Are they broken or cracked? Are they in working order? Of course, make sure they're clean. A little vinegar, water, and dish soap does wonders. Renting or hiring a company that does power washing is very easy and doesn't cost too much money. Again, you only have seconds to make a good impression, and you can only make a first impression once—make it count!

Does the front door need a fresh coat of paint? Plant fresh flowers to add color to the flower beds, and make sure the grass has been recently mowed and the trees are trimmed. Don't forget the side yards and the back yard. If the weather is warmer, consider having a beach chair or maybe some lemonade on the table, or have a small bistro set on the porch or patio—something that says to the buyers, "I want to spend my time here." Think of the buyers as your guests, people you like, and you want them to feel welcome and at home. Don't forget the outdoor lighting. Make sure they're not full of cobwebs, dead bugs, or burnt out light bulbs. Speaking of cobwebs, there's nothing worse than walking up to a home and finding that the doorbell and entrance is covered with cobwebs. It only takes seconds to give a bad impression. OK, we like what we see so far, but what the heck is that smell? Did something die?

Odors

It may seem like purchasing a home is all about the appearance, but you shouldn't underestimate the power of smell when it comes to the overall impact in showing your home. Instead of leaving this invisible factor up to chance, consider giving the house a quick, light spray with a pleasant scent, or even baking something that will be sure to remind potential buyers of the familiar comforts of home. Make sure you don't overdo it though; having too much scent may make potential buyers uncomfortable or even sick. A homeowner I was working with had plug-in air scents in every outlet throughout the home. Both agents and buyers were concerned why there were so many. Was the seller trying to cover something up? No matter how many times the seller got the feedback, the plug-ins stayed, turning off many buyers and agents.

Offensive odors are something lots of homeowners don't even know they have. We get so used to our own smells, we don't even notice there are offensive odors in our home. If you have any type of pet—cats, dogs, hamsters, ferrets, birds— you have odors. If you smoke, you have odors. If you cook with spices, you have odors. If you cook fish, you have odors. So, basically, if you cook, you have odors. Once your home is on the market, stop smoking inside, and stop cooking with strong smelling spices. An easy, breezy thing to do is to open the windows and let the home air out. If you're a heavy smoker, you may need to wash the walls, clean the light fixtures, and clean the windows. Don't forget to remove the ashtrays. If you have pets, then the odor is a little harder to get rid of. Consider having a friend or family member pet sit at their home. If that's not possible, then be sure to keep the bird cage clean, empty the kitty litter box, sweep, and vacuum the animal hair. By now, you're probably wondering what else could be the easiest, quickest, least expensive, and *biggest bang for the buck* improvement you can do. I'm so glad you asked—that great tip is coming up in the next section.

Paint/Decorate

Simple things often make a big difference. You can change the entire look and feel of a room by just changing the window treatments. New drapes or blinds add warmth and appeal and will instantly give your home a fresh new look.

If that's not enough, a fresh coat of paint will transform any room. Paint is one of the least expensive, biggest *bang for your buck* home decorating tools, but only if you do it right. Think of a high-end hotel and how they want you to stay longer and keep returning. Look in magazines for ideas. Just be sure to use calming, neutral colors— nothing too bold or over the top. If you have the patience, time and talent, you can save even more money by doing it yourself instead of hiring a professional painter.

If your furniture looks tired, try adding a slipcover, or new throw pillows in vibrant colors that either match or contrast your room's color scheme. This can make a world of difference and help your old furniture regain its appeal.

Bathrooms are the second most commonly remodeled room in the house (after the kitchen), but it can cost a lot of money to replace cabinets, fixtures, tile, or a tub. A quick and inexpensive tip is to get new towels and repaint the walls. Re-grout any tiled areas. Simple things can help give your bathroom a facelift: for the master bath, try adding candles, (there are some very nice flameless candles); fill the tub and add bubbles; play some soothing music; make it into a private retreat. A full, bubble-filled tub is inviting, and it keeps people from climbing into the tub with their shoes on.

Don't forget the small but meaningful things. Do the next tip wrong, and a buyer may want to negotiate down the price; do it right, and they won't have a leg to stand on.

Maintenance

Maintenance on a home is something that can really help your house sell faster and for more money. When the buyer and their agent are looking around the home, not only are they looking at the flow and floor plan of the home, but they're also looking for things that may be damaged or broken. More than likely, the buyer is going to have a home inspection.

Having taken care of the home and all the necessary repairs can considerably reduce the chances of the home inspector finding issues. Of course, no home is 100% perfect, not even new construction. And the inspector is sure to find something, anything to add to their report. You just don't want to give them too many items on their list and have the buyer negotiate money off the price, or have you, the homeowner, make the necessary repairs or, worse yet, the buyer walks away from the deal.

Maintaining the heating, ventilating, and cooling (HVAC) systems, and the plumbing, as well as the exterior and interior of the home, goes a long, long way toward getting your home sold faster and for more money. Central air conditioning, or window air conditioning units, are great selling features, but only if they work. If they look like they are on their last legs, it will adversely affect the sale.

You may have a 20-year-old boiler; however, if it's well maintained, clean, and you have all the service records, it won't be as much of an issue as having a 10-year-old boiler that looks like its 100 years old, hasn't been maintained, and there aren't service records, which then becomes a concern for the buyer.

You can relieve most buyers' concerns by simply having all the maintenance records, receipts for any major expenses, utility bills, and copies of service contracts on hand; this way the buyer knows they are purchasing a home that has been lovingly maintained and cared for. This one tip can get your home sold, not only faster than your competition but for more money. If you're selling your home, wouldn't you want a faster sale and more money in your pocket?

CHAPTER 3
HOW TO PRICE YOUR HOME

You are going to be so happy once you read this chapter. I say *happy* because, after reading this chapter, you will have more money in your bank account. That's a pretty bold statement. It's also a true statement. After reading this chapter, you will have more knowledge than 95% of home sellers. You will also make more demands on your Realtor® and will be more involved in the sale of your home.

"What do you think my house is worth? How much can I get for it? My neighbor said he got XXX for his, and I know my house is so much nicer than his." These are usually the first questions homeowners ask me.

Although these might seem like quick, simple questions, they really are anything but that. If you know this one leg of the process, you can sell your house quicker and easier, and get to the closing table with less hassles than your competition. I call it just one leg; however, there are several parts that comprise this leg. Let's start with the county data.

I'll use my county and town as an example. Don't worry if my numbers are different than your area; your local real estate agent can provide you with the correct data for your locale.

I live and work in Suffolk County, New York; that's the eastern county on Long Island, and the stats are provided by the local Multiple Listing Service of Long Island.

I want you to understand the following terms: *listings taken; under contract; sold;* and *days on the market*—in that order.

The first stat to consider is *listings taken* in Suffolk County, in the years, 2013, 2014, 2015, 2016.

Listings taken: in 2013 were 20,285; in 2014, there were 20,565; 2015, 22,237; and in 2016, there were 20,932.

As you can see, the amount of new listings that came on the market increased year over year, with the exception of 2016.

Next, let's consider *under contracts* for Suffolk County:

2013: 10,926; 2014: 10,322; 2015: 12,382; and up to June 2016: 14,467.

Moving right along to *closings* in Suffolk County:

2013: 10,172; 2014: 10,462; 2015: 11,101; and 2016: 13,355.

Let's talk about *days on market,* or DOM, as some people say. This stat is how long it takes from the time the listing hits the market until it is in full contract. I must remind you, these numbers are provided by the Multiple Listing Service of Long Island; your numbers may be very different. I just want you to have the concept so you can have an intelligent conversation with your Realtor®.

2013: 128; 2014: 123; 2015: 117; and 2016: 111.

I'm going to use Patchogue, New York, because this is where my office is located, and I had to pick a town. Again, I want you to understand the concept, not the exact numbers.

Right now, at this moment, there are 78 homes available in Patchogue, New York. If we break down the months prior, and what has sold in each month, we see:

Patchogue Available Inventory	78
Sold July 2016	15
Sold August 2016	31
Sold September 2016	28
Sold October 2016	23
Sold November 2016	26
Sold December 2016	25
Sold January 2017	16
Sold February 2017	13
Sold March 2017	14
Sold April 2017	15
Sold May 2017	24
Sold June 2017	25
Months' supply	4
% of homes selling (1 out of 4)	25.0%

This means Patchogue has a 4-month supply of homes on the market—it's a sellers' market. If no other homes came on the market, it would take 4 months to sell the existing inventory. Of course, we know that will never happen because, before I could finish writing this paragraph, more and more homes are coming up for sale. If we should look at a town such as Remsenburg, where the available inventory is 41, it might sound a bit low compared to Patchogue at 78; however, the month with the most sold homes in Remsenburg was a tie between January and June with 5 sales, and the least amount of sales, at 1, was May 2017. Remsenburg has a 13-month supply of homes—1 out of 13 or 7.7 %—giving buyers an upper hand.

Remsenburg Available Inventory	41
Sold August 2016	3
Sold September 2016	4
Sold October 2016	2
Sold November 2016	2
Sold December 2016	4
Sold January 2017	5
Sold February 2017	2
Sold March 2017	4
Sold April 2017	2
Sold May 2017	1
Sold June 2017	5
Sold July 2017	3
Months' Supply	13
% of Homes Selling (1 out of 13)	7.7%

So, what can you do about it? Well, first off, market your home to be *IN* the market, not *ON* the market. If you don't do this, you will be helping your competition sell *their* house, while you wait and wait for someone, or anyone, to buy your house. If you're reading this book, I doubt you're the type of person who wants to help your competition.

So, what exactly do I mean by *IN* the market vs *ON* the market? Knowing this one marketing strategy will propel you from listing your home, to getting offers, to the closing table, leaving your competition in the dust and wondering how you did it. When a home is *ON* the market, it's overpriced, it has a low commission, it's not offering closing costs for the buyer, it's not offering a home warranty, and it's not holding a mortgage. I'm not saying you need to offer all of the above. As a matter of fact, I have a guaranteed checklist system to get my homeowners to the closing table faster and with more money in their pocket— I'm sure that's something you would like to know how to do. It's called the marketability checklist, and this is how it works: There are 20 items on the list. In the Patchogue market, where we have a 4-month supply, the homeowner would need to have at least 14 of the 20 items on the list. A homeowner in

Remsenburg would need all 20, since they have a 13-month supply.

Marketability check list	Yes	No
1. Awesome Realtor®		
2. Below market price		
3. Yard sign		
4. Owner financing		
5. Home warranty		
6. Accessible		
7. Move in condition (exterior)		
8. Move in condition (interior)		
9. Full term listing		
10. Pre-ordered appraisal		
11. Pre-ordered inspection		
12. Quick possession		
13. Seller to complete obvious repairs		
14. Appliances and extras included		
15. No contingencies		
16. Lease purchase		
17. Post-dated price reduction		
18. Above average commission		
19. Search friendly sales price		
20. Seller to pay closing costs		
Total		

The second one on the list, below market price, can sometimes worry a homeowner: "I'm not giving my house away!" I get it—I really do—just stay with me for a minute while I explain. If you're like most homeowners, you think pricing your home above what it is worth will get you more money. I thought the exact same way before I became a Realtor® and saw how it really worked. Let's say your home is worth around 500K—it might be higher or lower, but I had to pick a number, so let's go with it. By pricing it at just 10% above market value, at 550K, only 30% of buyers will even look at your home. "Not bad," you say, "Thirty percent sounds good." I say it's terrible. That means 70% of potential qualified buyers are NOT seeing your home. And if you go 15% above market value, then a mere pittance of 10% of buyers will be looking at your home. That's not many buyers to negotiate with on the price and terms of sale of your home. Now, here is the good news, and the way successful homeowners negotiate the best price and terms for their home, allowing them to get to the closing table sooner and with more money in their pocket. Some people say you need guts to do this, but I say you don't need guts to use the smartest strategy you can. If you price your home just 10% below market value, you will have 75% of buyers looking at your home. On a 500K house, that means we would price it at 450K. Buyers will be comparing your home to other homes priced around 450K, and they will find more value in your home. We all know the value of supply and demand—it drives prices up like crazy. Whenever I have serious homeowners that use this strategy, we get multiple offers, allowing us to select the best buyer with the best price and terms, and eliminating having to negotiate with only 1 buyer. When pricing your home, look at the list of homes that are similar to yours in number of bedrooms, baths, style, etc., and position yourself in the top percent that are selling for your town.

By using the 19 strategies you can go from being one of the 78 available and *ON* the market, to soaring to the top 1 in 4 homes that are *IN* the market and *SOLD.* We'll go over what makes an offer a good offer, in another chapter.

For more things to consider when selling your house, go to:

www.SellYourHouseBook.com

and leave the competition in the dust....

CHAPTER 4

HOME PRICES: WHERE ARE THEY?

WHERE ARE THEY GOING?

If you're like me and love numbers, you're going to love this chapter; if you're the type of person who doesn't like numbers, stay with me anyway because this is a powerful chapter that plays a huge part in not only pricing your home but also in selecting the right agent to work with. So many times, an agent will skip over this material, or the homeowner just doesn't care. I find skipping this information to be a big mistake in knowing how to price your home. I compare it to needing surgery, and the patient tells the doctor, "Just do what you need to do. I just want to sleep through it, and I don't want to know anything about the procedure." Although you may not understand everything the doctor is telling you, isn't it better to be educated on the surgery so you can make an informed decision? If your real estate agent isn't at least trying to discuss the following information with you, get a new agent. I'm serious about that. Just like you would find a new doctor that *does* explain the procedure, you shouldn't work with an agent that either can't, or worse, doesn't know about the national trends. So, let's dive right in and talk about *mortgage rates.*

Mortgage Rates

The all-time high interest rate was in 1981 at a staggering 18.63%. The monthly payment for principal and interest was $3,177 on a $200,000 fully amortizing mortgage. If we travel back in time to the all-time low in November 2012, the rate was 3.31%. Taking that same loan from 1981, our payment would be just $877 per month. That's a difference of $2300 per month, or $27,600 a year. I don't know about you, but I would be ecstatic saving $2300 a month on my mortgage. The 2Q of 2017 interest rates were 4.0%, and Freddie Mac is saying interest rates are going up by more than a point by this time next year.

* Information Provided by Keeping Current Matters

Let's look at examples of 3 different price points:

With an interest rate of just 3.75% on a $500,000 home, the principal and interest payment would be around $2,316 a month. If rates go up just a quarter of a percent, that brings the payment up to $2,327, thereby reducing the buying power by –2.5%, or a purchase price of $487,500. If rates go up a full percent to 4.75%, that same $500,000 house will cost $2,347 a month, reducing the buying power by –10%, making it a $450,000 purchase.

Our second example is a sales price of $700,000 with an interest rate of 3.75%. The principal and interest payment would be around $3,242 a month. With just a small, quarter percent increase, the payment goes up to $3,258, thereby reducing the buying power by –2.5%, or a purchase price of $682,500. Take that same sales price of $700,000 with just a 1% interest increase, and the payment goes up to $3,286 a month, thereby reducing the buying power by –10%, or a purchase price of $630,000.

Our third example is a house with a list price of $1,000,000. At the same interest rate of 3.75%, the monthly payment of principal and interest would be $4,631. With a quarter percent interest increase, the new payment is

$4,654, thereby reducing the buying power by -2.5%, or a purchase price of $975,000. With a full 1% increase in interest rates, the payment becomes $4,695, or a purchase price of $900,000, which is 10% below the original list price of $1,000,000.

That's huge! And it's only a 1% increase. If Fannie Mae's, Freddie Mac's, MBA's, and NAR's combined projection of mortgage rates for 2017 3Q are correct, the rate will be 4.37%. I think you're starting to get the picture about the impact that increasing interest rates have on buying power and how you need to know this when selling your home. *

If you are moving to a higher priced home, you can see how the interest rates play a big role in the dollar amount of house you can purchase; the same principles apply to selling a lower priced home.

If you would like current mortgage rates and data on a buyer's purchasing power, and additional helpful information, visit: SellYourHouseBook.com.

Information provided by Keeping Current Matters

Resale Homes, Inventory, Sales and Prices

Let's look at inventory for 3 categories: starter homes, trade up homes, and premium homes (where they were in 2012 compared to today, in 2016.)

Starting with inventory levels

Inventory for starter homes is extremely low, with only 234K in 2016, compared to 432K in 2012—that's about a 54.5% drop in inventory. This is a huge deal; so big that it slows down the sales of all 3 categories. With the slowdown of sales for starter homes, those current owners won't be able to purchase a larger home, which in turn clogs the top tier from progressing.

Along the same path of the starter home, is the trade up home. Inventory is down to 225K in 2016, compared to 380K in 2012; that's about a 60% drop in just 4 years.

You may be happy to hear premium homes are on a different trajectory. 2012 had only 225K homes for sale vs the 398K we have in 2016; that's a 56% increase over 4 years.

Year Over Year Price Changes by Category

Bottom tier homes are up in price by 7.9%, middle tier homes are up by 5.4%, and top tier homes are up by only 4%, which means if you're an owner with a top tier home, you have to be even more accurate with the list price of your home for it to stand out from your competition and fight for those few buyers.

Although 93% of Americans believe homeownership is something to be proud of, and 86% see homeownership as a dream come true, I believe one of the reasons inventory for starter homes is low is because first-time homebuyers are not recognizing the value in owning a home. It's either because of that or they mistakenly believe, in order to qualify for a mortgage, you need at least 20% down, which is not the case.

IPSOS conducted a study that revealed 40% of the population believes you need at least 20% down to purchase a home. Can you imagine the impact if the 40% of the population started buying homes? Even if only 10% started buying a home, it would create a huge shift in sales.

On top of the 40% of the population being

misinformed about the down payment, the senior vice president of Ellie Mae, Jonas Moe, said, "The high, median credit scores are due to many millennials believing they won't qualify with the score they have, and are waiting to apply for a mortgage when they have the score they think they need." The average FICO score is in the low 720s. The masses believe they need a credit score of 780 or better to qualify for a mortgage. According to Ellie Mae, in regard to the FICO score distribution of loans closed, 54.9% of buyers had a FICO score of 600–749, with 700–749 having 24% share. Borrowers with a FICO score of 750–799 made up 31.9%, and a FICO score of over 800 was only 12.8% of all loans. The average FICO score for all loans was 724, and if we break it down by loan type: conventional 754; FHA 686; and VA 707.

* Information provided by Keeping Current Matters

We took a look at inventory; now, let's look at existing home sales, year-over-year by region, July 2016:

According to the National Association of Realtors (NAR), every region had an increase in sales, with the exception of the West. The Midwest had an increase of 3.2%, the South 6.5%, the Northeast 11.6%, and the West had a decrease of 1.7%—overall, the US had an increase of 4.5%.

Take a look at NEW home sales by price range:

Under 150K up 4%

150–199K up 14%

200–299K up 33%

300–399K up 24%

400–499K up 9%

500–749K up 10%

750K, and above, up 6%

Home Prices

Let's look at what NAR has to say about existing home prices, year over year by region:

The US, overall, is up 4.7%; the Northeast has taken a hit with -0.1%; the West is up 7.7%; the South is up 5.9%; and the Midwest is up by 4.6%.

% change in sales from 2015 to 2016 by price range:

Every price range over 100K has increased dramatically, with the midrange 250–500K having the biggest jump. Here is the breakdown according to NAR:

0–100K down by –1.6%
100–250K up by 8.2%
250–500K up by 17.1%
500–750K up by 16.5
750–1M up by 15%
1M+ up by 12%

The appraisal can be affected by the quick rise in home prices. If a home is priced at 200K and the appraisal is off by just 2%, it means there is a shortage of 4K; that can be a huge challenge for both the homeowner and buyer who is already nervous about buying a house.

For current data on where prices are and where they're going, along with other helpful information, visit: Sellyourhousebook.com

I'm so excited for you! You are now about 90% smarter than the average home seller. And for even more up-to-date stats, along with other helpful information, visit:

Sellyourhousebook.com

CHAPTER 5
HOW TO FIND THE PERFECT REALTOR®
FOR YOU

A little unknown but important distinction is that all agents are not Realtors®—all Realtors® are not the same! A great Realtor® can be your best asset when selling your home; their market knowledge, industry relationships, and negotiating skills can have a huge impact on your final sales price!

A Realtor® is someone who not only has more education, but also adheres to the strict code of ethics and standards of practice of the National Association of Realtors® (NAR). Just because someone has their real estate license does not automatically make them a Realtor®. A broker is a person who has taken the initiative to educate themselves beyond the salesperson, they have passed the state brokers exam. A broker can either work alone or they can hire agents to work for them.

So, what is the best way to find a real estate agent?

Maybe you already know a real estate agent. Do you like their personality? Are they someone you can trust with one of the largest assets you will ever own? If for some reason you're not happy with the way things are going, can you see yourself firing them? Should you look online? In your neighborhood? Ask your friends and family? Co-workers? Should you use the agent your friend used? After all, the house did sell. What about the agent on that billboard you pass every day? You remember getting a postcard last week; what was that agent's name? What about going to an open house? What about a small Mom and Pop company vs a global company? How will you know if they're the right agent for you? Will they understand your situation? How does all of this work? Will they answer all of your questions? These are just some of the questions homeowners ask themselves before starting the process. Here are some of the most common ways of going about finding the right real estate agent for you.

We'll get into the questions and demands you should make on your real estate agent a little later in the chapter; first, let's discuss the 5 most common ways of finding the right agent for you.

Referral

The first is the most obvious, and that is to ask family and friends. We do this all the time in our everyday life; we ask for a recommendation to a great restaurant, dry cleaner, school, landscaper, type of car, etc. When asking family and friends for a recommendation, be sure to ask how they chose their agent and what they liked or didn't like about the agent. But don't stop there; you still need to do your due diligence and online research. As with all agents, or anyone you are working with for that matter, you need to like and trust them or, at the very least, feel in your gut that they are going to do the best job they can for you.

Advertisements

Signs, signs, everywhere signs. Now that you have decided to sell your home, I'm sure you have been noticing a ton of *for sale* signs you never noticed before. Is there 1 agent that has the lion share of signs? They could be the top listing agent in your area, or they could just be playing the numbers game. Yes, I'm sad to say that a small percentage of agents will tell you everything you want to hear. They will says things such as, "I can get you

100K over what the home is worth." They list, and list, and list homes, hoping and praying the odds are with them and, of course, some of the homes will sell. Too many agents just take the listing at any price and try to work the seller for a price correction later. Make them show you how and why they arrived at the price for your home; 24% of all real estate transactions have an issue with the appraisal, meaning it's becoming more difficult to get the banks to agree on the contract price. You may find a buyer willing to pay more than the appraised value of your home, but will they be able to get a mortgage? As a general rule, banks will not lend more than the appraised value of a home. Be sure your agent is discussing this with you at the time of the listing. The *top producing* agent will have a larger network of buyers due to the fact they are actually selling their clients' homes. With so many clients to service, a *top producer* may sometimes have some sort of help in the way of an assistant or team member.

On Line

It has become common to research anything on the Internet. You can Google an agent's name, company, or your town to find an agent. You can go to Zillow or realtor.com. There are literally hundreds of websites. Just be sure to verify any information you read on the Internet.

Open Houses

Another great way to find your perfect agent is to visit open houses. Before getting into the business, this is how we found our awesome agent. For us, one of the things we liked about her was that she didn't pester us for our listing like some other agents did after hearing we were thinking of selling our condo. She was more concerned with selling the home we were seeing that day, which told us she wouldn't be trying to recruit new clients at our open house if we hired her. I have obtained a lot of business from clients I have met at an open house; our personalities just clicked. Pay attention to how they go about their business. Are they pushy, or informative and pleasant? Are they well-informed about the home they are trying to sell? Do they know the local area?

Visit Your Local Real Estate Office

Of course, you can always call or visit the offices of a real estate company. This is actually a great way to get the first impression of the company and how they treat their clients. Is the receptionist welcoming and professional? Is the office clean? Do people seem busy, or are they just sitting around talking about the company picnic? Whether on the phone or in person, ask to speak with the manager about a recommendation of who they think would be the best agent for your needs. If the manager is unavailable at the time, then leave a message. If they don't get back to you within a reasonable time frame for you, then move on to the next office.

What to Look for in a Professional Agent

Now that you know where to find an agent, let's discuss what to look for. The National Association of Realtors® requires a minimum 22.5 hours of continuing education, every 2 years. Some agents know the value of furthering their education to serve their clients better by achieving designations and certifications, or obtaining their associate broker's license. My belief is to always look for an agent that goes beyond the bare minimum and is always striving to improve. Yes, they may have been in the business 10, 20, or 30 years but, as we all know, things can change dramatically over time; keeping up with the development of technology, and any changes or new laws, is extremely important. Using an agent that hasn't kept up with changing laws can hurt you, and might even get you in a bucket of hot water, and possibly sued—all because they couldn't be bothered taking an ethics class and didn't advise you correctly.

Ask for a copy of their marketing plan. How will they go about making sure your home gets the most exposure possible? After all, the more exposure, the greater the chance of finding the right buyer for your home. Who do they think will be the potential buyer for your home? Do they have a customizable marketing plan to attract those buyers? Will they explain any and all items on their plan, and the benefits to using them, or will they just say, "This is what I do; take it or leave it." Maybe they don't even have a written marketing plan, and they're hoping and praying, by putting up a sign, and having it on the multiple listing service, it will sell. I can't tell you how many times my clients are surprised when we review my written marketing plan with all its elements, and that it can be customized for each client's needs. Whatever you do, do not choose an agent who will take your listing and wait for the house to sell itself. Choose an agent with a plan to attract qualified buyers. Remember when I said all agents are not Realtors®, and all Realtors® are not the same? I'm sure you're starting to get the picture.

By paying close attention to the next factor, it will not only save you money but a heap of frustration.

A great question most homeowners neglect to ask is about communication. Maybe that's because they just don't know what an important role communication plays in the whole process. Does the agent have a written communication plan? I have to say, the odds of an agent having a communication plan is slim; and having a written communication plan—well, you're probably better off winning the lottery. Very, very few homeowners know to ask this question and, now that you know to ask, it will tell you if you have found the right agent. I hear this all the time from homeowners that tried to sell but got rejected by the market. Their most common complaint is that they never hear from their agent, and they didn't know the listing had expired. How sad is that? What makes that so unfortunate is the sellers not knowing anything else, and they think this is how all agents run their business. Knowing the communication process with an agent ahead of time can save you precious selling time when on the market. Some great questions to ask are: how often can you expect a phone call, an email, etc. from the agent? What is their response time? Three hours? Three days? Or, heaven forbid, three weeks! What is the number of their office, and the manager's name, in case you don't hear from the agent in an agreed upon time frame? If they are a *top producer,* will they be contacting you, or will you be speaking with an assistant, administrator or, perhaps a team member? Just like everyone else, real estate agents have a personal life; sometimes an emergency may arise when they are unavailable for a period of time, but there should be someone you can call to ask questions.

Personalities play a big role in the process; finding an agent with a personality you like is extremely important. After all, you will be working with this person for approximately 6–12 months, in what will most likely be an intense relationship. Trust your gut on this one. Who recommended them to you is not important; what is important is that you are comfortable with the agent, and you are confident they will take care of your needs in the sale of your home, and accomplish everything with professionalism. You're going to have to trust your gut. After all, your home is probably one of the largest assets you own, if not the largest asset.

Questions and Demands

Demands to make on your real estate agent:

Demand #1

Does the agent understand the timetable with which your family is dealing?

You will be moving your family to a new home. Whether the move revolves around the start of a new school year or the start of a new job, you will be trying to put the move to a plan. This can be emotionally draining, and having an agent that understands and appreciates the timetables is an invaluable asset. Your agent won't be able to pick the exact date of your move; however, they should exert any influence they can to make it work.

Demand #2

Remove as many of the challenges as possible.

It is imperative that your agent knows how to handle the challenges that will arise. An agent's ability to negotiate is critical. If you have an agent who is weak when negotiating with you on the parts of the listing contract that were most important to the seller and their family (fee, length of the listing, etc.), don't expect them to turn into a superhero negotiator when it comes to you and your family.

Demand #3

Get the house sold.

There is a reason you are putting yourself and your family through the process of moving.

You are moving on with your life in some way. The reason is important, or you wouldn't be dealing with the headaches and challenges that come along with selling. Do not allow your agent to forget these motivations. Constantly remind them that selling the house is why you hired them. Make sure that they don't worry about your feelings more than they worry about your family. If they discover some things that need to be done to attain your goal (e.g. price correction, repair, removing clutter), insist that they be 100% honest and have the courage to inform you.

Demand #4

Tell the truth about the price.

Remember earlier when I spoke about the agent playing the numbers game? This is the agent who will tell you any price, even if overpriced, just so they can get your business. They could also be the lowest bidder when it comes to discussing their fee. Some markets seem to encourage agents or companies to change their value proposition to a low listing fee. This is designed to generate a higher volume of business for them due to the perceived savings for the homeowner. The risk to you is in this business model. Because they are working on *volume*, and need to turn properties quickly due to their low profit margin, they can be less motivated to put in the work necessary to keep a difficult deal together. There is also little enthusiasm to work to get you the highest possible price and then deal with the appraisal challenges and potential buyer's remorse. Because of the complexities and risks of selling in a seller's market, you would probably benefit from an agent offering a competitive listing fee, and who would be a great resource for you to mitigate risk and any and all efforts needed to help you achieve your goals. I always have a discussion with my clients about the pros and cons of any fee. Most people have heard of the Pareto Principle, also known as the 80/20 rule. This rule states that 80% of results are attributed to 20% of the cause. In real estate, the numbers are slightly different. In real estate, 10% of the agents do 90% of the work, leaving 90% of agents to fight for 10% of the work. Read that sentence again. *Just* 10% of agents handle 90% of the work; they do 90% of the sales, and they make 90% of the income. *Just* 10%! That's amazing. One of the reasons is because some agents get into the business as part timers or hobbyists. These are usually the agents who will say anything and do anything to buy your listing; then, when they get back to the office, they sit at their desk with their hands together and pray that your house sells. They pray that one of the top 10% of the agents is on the other side of the deal because, either they don't know how to handle an issue should it arise, or they need to get back to their full-time job, and they put all the responsibilities and work in the top producer's lap.

Questions

Are they full time or part time? This should be in your top 5 questions. The odds of a real estate agent earning a living from selling real estate are low. Due to the attrition rate of around 97% in year 1, many agents start their career in real estate part time. Maybe, in the beginning, a friend or family member needed help selling or buying a home, and the agent found it to be a great way to earn a little extra cash. Usually, once they find out how hard they have to work to get a paycheck, and all the fees involved, they gravitate towards a steady paycheck. Then again, I know plenty of agents who are successful in their part time real estate career. This is most likely because they treat it as a job and not as a hobby. If they're able to meet your needs in selling your home, and you have a good feeling about the agent, then go ahead and hire them.

Asking what percentage of the agents listings sold last year is a great question and something that's easy to verify. If an agent is listing X amount of homes but only 10% of them sold, then that should be a red flag to you. Being careful about the agent that brags about their success, or their company's success, should be an important consideration when deciding on the right real estate professional to represent you in the sale of your home. Be sure the agent is interested in establishing your needs; how successful they may seem, or how many awards they have, is much less important than you and your family's needs.

What experience does the agent have in selling homes in your area or price range?

This is another great question to ask during your interview. You'll want to know if a particular agent has any experience selling homes in your area or close by.

Although this is not essential to a successful sale, it could be a factor. Many successful agents do not specialize in a neighborhood or area; they often find themselves working across a large metro area because their business has been built on developing lasting relationships based on professional and ethical service, and they, therefore, receive referrals from past clients that take them to different neighborhoods.

Something that very rarely comes up is the topic of open houses. The subject of open houses should be discussed during the marketing plan and communication conversation. Some of the first questions should be: do you want to have open houses? How often? What day of the week is best? What time of day? Who will be hosting the open house? What do you need to do to prepare for an open house? How often should you have an open house? How will the open house be advertised? A great agent will explain everything and review the pros and cons with you. Some homeowners mistakenly think that having an open house every weekend for 5–6 hours is a great idea, and that it gives the buyers ample time to view the home. However, in actuality, it can hurt them when the time comes to negotiate, and they might even get a low offer. By being so available, you're telling the buyers to *please, please come see my home. Please stop by and buy my home.* On the other hand, if you have an open house every couple of weeks for 1–2 hours, a buyer who is really interested in your home will rearrange their schedule to accommodate the time, giving you the upper hand. So many homeowners think they will start receiving offers at the first open house. Although this does happen sometimes, it is rare. If I have a home that I think will be in high demand, I will restrict all showings until the first open house. We collect the names and contact information of all the agents and public who inquired about the home. We let them know showings will start on such and such a date and time; if they are really interested, they will make it a priority. We've had buyers be the first ones at the open house, place their offer, and not leave until it was over, ensuring they would be the purchasers. Now, before you get too excited, remember this is rare; you need to have an extremely desirable property to get the results and, even then, it may not happen. Also, please don't think having an open house is like what you see on some of the TV shows, where they have tons and tons of people show up. That's TV, and that rarely happens in real life.

So many times, buyers are just curious about a home but aren't quite ready to pull the trigger, so they will do a softer approach and visit open houses to get a better feel of what they're looking for. Then, if they are really interested, they will schedule an appointment for a private showing.

CHAPTER 6
All THE HARD WORK HAS PAID OFF.
YOU HAVE AN OFFER

Is it a good offer or a bad offer? What makes it a good offer? How will you know? Most homeowners want the highest, best price for their house, and this is perfectly understandable. However, the highest price might not necessarily be the best offer.

Every home seller has a different situation and different needs. Maybe you just got an awesome promotion with your company; the only glitch is that it's across the country and you need to be there in six months. What do you do? Or you just found out your family is rapidly growing—your wife is pregnant with triplets. There is no way you can all fit in your small house anymore. As you can see, it not only depends on your motivation but also price and terms.

Price and Terms

It all comes down to price and terms. So many times, a seller will focus on only the price and disregard the terms. Doing this can be a huge mistake.

Let's say a buyer offered to pay you full price for your home. You're excited and elated—but wait, there's just one little hiccup. Before you can call the movers, you find out the buyer won't be able to close for at least twelve months. Is it still a good offer for you? Are you willing to wait a year for your money? You're probably thinking that would never happen; I'm here to tell you it happens more often than you realize. This is when we start to get into the domino effect. The domino effect is when your buyer is selling their home, and the purchase of your home is predicated on the sale of their home. Not only do you need your buyer to have everything in place, but also your buyer's buyer. As you can see, it can be challenging to coordinate the many, many steps. What if you had a buyer who was offering less for your home but could close quickly; they could close in your timeframe, thereby allowing you to move into your dream home or take that big promotion. I'm sure you can see how having a team of professionals on your side, to help you navigate through the maze of all the different stages, is critical.

There are a number of factors that comprise an offer. The first question usually is: is it cash or a mortgage? Now, you might be thinking, "Well, if it's cash, that great! I can start packing." Not so fast—a cash offer may have its drawbacks. But you're saying, "Cash is king." In this case, yes and no. Yes, you will usually be able to close quickly with a cash offer; however, it could mean less money in your pocket and, in some cases, as much as 10%, 20%, 30%, or sometimes even 50% below your asking price. Why would a buyer paying cash want such a steep discount? Because they know there's no waiting for an appraisal or waiting for the bank to do their due diligence. You will be able to get to the closing table sooner than someone taking out a mortgage and, depending on your personal situation, you may need to get out today or, sometimes, yesterday. So, ask yourself: would you rather have less money quicker, or get more money but have to wait due to a longer timeframe for the mortgage process.

As you can see, understanding price and terms can make a significant difference.

Lucky for you, your home is the number one selling home—a ranch. It has three bedrooms and 1 and a half baths, a full basement, and a one car garage. This was your first home, and you love the home; however, your family is growing and you need more space, so you have decided to sell and move up to the home of your dreams—the perfect, large Victorian you saw over the weekend. This home checked all the boxes on your list: it has enough bedrooms; it has enough baths; it has a beautiful master suite with large walk in closets; and it has a beautifully maintained backyard that looks like something straight out of a magazine. You picture yourself entertaining your friends and having a blast in this perfect home. But before you can buy that perfect home, you first need to sell your current home.

Imagine for a minute that you have multiple offers. How can you decide which is best for you?

I'm sure you're familiar with the Ben Franklin way to make a decision like this; just go over the pros and cons of each offer.

- Offer #1 – The buyers don't have a home to sell, which, in your case, is good because you can't afford to wait.

After all, someone is going to scoop up that picture-perfect home you like so much. The offer isn't full price; however, they are pre-approved for a conventional mortgage with a bank you and your agent don't recognize. The buyers can accommodate your schedule but would rather close ASAP. Their offer is 10% below asking price.

- Offer #2 – The buyers have a home to sell, and the offer is a lot lower than you would like. They are only putting down 3.5%, which means they have to mortgage 96.5%. Again, just like the first offer, your agent can negotiate a better price for you. They are pre-approved for an FHA mortgage with a reputable bank that both you and your agent know very well. They're flexible about a closing date since their home is already under contract and they are able to stay with family during the transition. This might make it easier for your family to move from your home right into that picture perfect Victorian. Their offer is 5% below asking price.

- Offer #3 – The buyer is all cash. Cash is great because you won't have to worry about any bank requirements. Just like the other two buyers, this buyer will have a home inspection. The only other requirement is a clear title. Your agent has the proof of funds and has verified its authenticity. Because of the convenience of a cash purchase, the closing can take place in 2–4 weeks, but the price is the lowest of all the offers. It's 20% below asking price.

You probably noticed that none of the buyers offered the full asking price. Don't be insulted that no one offered you full price. Most times, a buyer wants to feel like they got a good deal on their purchase. After all, I bet you weren't going to offer full price on the home you have your eye on—were you?

Also, if you did receive a full price offer, it doesn't mean your home was priced too low. What it really means is that you priced it to sell, and the buyers were probably already in the market looking and maybe missed out on some homes. When they saw your home, they didn't want to waste any time.

Do you counter all three offers, or just negotiate with one or two? What will you do?

The first thing is to sit down with your real estate agent and prioritize which items are most important to you and your family's needs. Is it price? Timeframe? An unencumbered buyer? Terms of a mortgage? FHA vs conventional? Does your home meet FHA guidelines? Is it a reputable bank?

Did you already pick your buyer from the 3 examples? If a hundred people were asked which buyer is the right buyer, a hundred people would give a different answer, and all for different reasons.

There is no rule or guideline that you have to accept any of the 3 offers. You can say you don't like any of them, or that you only want to counter the cash buyer because you need to sell quickly and you like the fact that a bank isn't involved in the transaction.

After having a conversation with your Realtor®, you counter two of the three offers and come to an agreement.

Don't start packing just yet. Although you are on your way, there are some steps we need to address first.

In the next chapter, you will find out the step by step process of actually selling your home.

CHAPTER 7

UNDERSTANDING THE CLOSING PROCESS

Sales Binder

The sales binder is sometimes called the sales agreement or, simply, binder. Sometimes a buyer will make a verbal offer, and your agent might insist they put it in writing so you know they're serious. A sales binder contains:

- The buyer's name and address
- Seller's name and address
- The address of the home the buyer is purchasing
- Offer amount
- Amount down at contract
- Amount of down payment
- Amount of mortgage or cash
- Dates as to when the buyer would like to be in full contract

- Date buyer will obtain their mortgage commitment, if applicable
- Date and signature of the buyer
- The type of mortgage (FHA, VA, Conventional, etc.)
- The pre-approval letter or proof of funds (should accompany the sales agreement)
- Pending home inspection clause, or some other similar clause

Amount down on contract and *amount of down payment* are not the same things. Although the amount down at contract varies from place to place, what doesn't vary is the buyer trying to put down the least amount possible, just in case something should change; they would rather have less money on the table to worry about. I've been trained on filling out the binder in a way that gets my clients the most money for their house. No, I don't fill in the blank lines afterwards or do anything underhanded; it's all in what and how I say things to the buyer. I cannot share this secret here; some things must remain a secret for my clients' best interest.

The sales agreement usually includes a clause for *home inspection* and *subject to the buyer obtaining a mortgage*.

Hopefully, by this time, you have already spoken to an attorney and made them aware you will be selling your home and that they should expect communication from your real estate agent.

Once you have an accepted offer, your agent will take the sales agreement, along with any other necessary paperwork, and send it over to your attorney. When your attorney receives all the paperwork, they will review everything and give you a call if they have any questions. They will then draw up the contracts. Once your attorney draws up the contract, it is then sent to the buyer's attorney to review. If everything is what they expected, and any changes don't affect them dramatically, then the buyer will make an appointment to sign the contract and bring the agreed amount of monies due at signing. This money is held by the seller's attorney in a separate escrow account. At this point, you are in half contract. Then, the attorney for the buyer will send the contract to your attorney, and then you can go in and sign. Once you sign, you are in full contract.

Good Faith Money

One item that is no longer practiced in my area is the *good faith money* deposit, also known as earnest money deposit, or contract deposit. Although there is still a line for it on the sales agreement, this practice is obsolete in my area, and may be in your area as well. Good faith money gave the buyers the ability to put a small deposit on a home, maybe $100 or so; however, it was usually never large enough for the seller to take it seriously.

Escrow/Down Payment Money

Escrow money, also known as down payment money, is held in a separate account by the seller's attorney and is credited to the buyer at closing. Attorney, Robert Caputo, of Smithtown, NY, states that an attorney must hold monies in a separate account, or face stiff penalties by the bar association. Any co-mingling of monies is strictly forbidden.

Home and Termite Inspection

The vast majority of today's buyers are conducting home inspections before they purchase a home.

Depending on where you live, the inspection could be done before you are in full contract, or after. Your Realtor® can advise on your local customs.

Depending on the size of your home, an inspection can take anywhere from 1–5 hours, and sometimes even more if it's a very large home.

Inspectors

Nowadays, it's very common for purchasers to require a home inspection before purchasing a home. I remember when we bought our first home. The real estate agent was a friend of the family and said he found the perfect home for us. All it needed was a downspout and a little painting. At that time, it was unusual for buyers to spend the money on a home inspection. I might be showing my age by saying this, but think of a wedding in the 70s or 80s, when couples rarely had a videographer. Now, the couples not only have a photographer but several photographers, a videographer, a DJ, maybe a DJ with a drummer, and sometimes a DJ with a band. So, we didn't think anything of it when our agent told us not to waste our money on a home inspection. That one mistake, on our part, cost us thousands and thousands of dollars, so don't be surprised if the buyers request a home inspection.

When the inspection will take place, depends on where you live. Here, on Long Island, it's customary to have the inspection immediately after the buyer and seller agree on price and terms but before contracts are drawn up. We once had an offer accepted on a Saturday afternoon; the buyers were so eager to get the home under contract, we had the inspection at 7 a.m. the following morning. Thank goodness, the buyer's agent and homeowner were all onboard and could accommodate the early hour. Other parts of the country have the home inspection after the contracts are signed. It's best to ask your real estate professional about your local practice.

Who attends the home inspection? Usually, the buyers and their agent, your agent, and sometimes some friends or family of the buyers and, of course, the inspector.

The purpose of the home inspection, obviously, is to find out if the house is structurally sound, has any defects, and if the plumbing, electrical, and HVAC systems are in proper working order and up to code. According to John

Zeoli, of New Home Inspections, an inspection is not to pick apart the house; it's simply to verify the home is a sound investment for the buyer.

Here is a list of just some of the items you can expect to be checked:

- Roof, including shingles, flashing, and skylights
- Structural foundation and framing
- Electrical system, circuit breakers and fuses, electrical outlets
- Plumbing, drains, water heaters
- HVAC systems
- Insulation and venting system in the attic and other unfinished spaces
- Siding, soffits, railings, decks, windows, porches, and balconies
- Doors, stairs
- Appliances
- Fireplaces, chimneys, vents
- Possibly a termite inspection

Depending on the size of the home, an inspection can take anywhere from 1–5 hours. I remember when I was selling a vacant, 1-bedroom co-op. The whole place consisted of a kitchen, living room, bathroom, and bedroom. It took 2 inspectors almost 2 hours to complete the inspection—on a little one bedroom co-op. I had to wonder if they dragged out the inspection to make the buyer believe they were getting their money's worth.

After the inspection is completed, the inspector might walk the buyer around the home and point out any concerns. Then, he/she will send a report to the buyer about their findings.

If the buyer is satisfied with the report, contracts can be sent out. If something should arise that is not up to code or the buyer doesn't like, then those items can be negotiated, or the buyer may decide it's not the home for them. This is where a great real estate agent and attorney can use their knowledge to help keep the deal together. Sometimes something might be able to be taken care of and is not a big deal; however, to the novice buyer or home seller, it seems like the end of the deal.

Title Search

Title search is an extremely important step in the selling of your home.

Whether the buyer is mortgage or cash, their attorney will most likely order a title search, which is the chain of different owners of the property. This makes sure no one will come forward and stake a claim to the property, and it also ensures there aren't any open permits or liens against the property. Depending on where you live, this could take anywhere from a couple of days to months and months. Sometimes there are buildings on a property without proper Certificate of Occupancy, or permits. The attorney may have to reach people who can remember when the building was constructed, and sign a sworn affidavit to the fact. This isn't as easy as it sounds—people move, and memories fade. As you can see, there can be a lot of gray matter; nothing is usually black and white.

Once you get through the sales agreement, home inspection, and contract signing...

If the buyer is obtaining a mortgage, it's time for the bank to start their due diligence. Just like you, they want to be sure the purchase is a sound decision.

The bank will order an appraisal of the home to make sure it is worth the amount of the purchase price. Of course, this step is omitted if you have a cash buyer.

The appraisal is noninvasive and, depending on the size of the home, can take anywhere from 15 minutes (maybe even less) to 30 or 40 minutes. The appraiser will take both interior and exterior photos, along with a street view. Then, they will get a copy of the survey and floor plan (if available), and look at other similar homes that have sold, in order to come up with a price for the bank.

What will you do if the appraised value is lower than the banks value? You have several options: sell at the appraised value; have the buyer bring the difference to the closing table; both you and the buyer kick in some money to help the sale go through; or walk away from the sale and start from scratch. Your attorney will be able to help you make the right decision for you.

You're probably wondering who pays for what. Since I don't know where you live, I will just list the customary fees in my area. Your Realtor® or attorney will be more familiar with the fees in your area.

You pay for your own attorney—makes sense, right? The buyer pays for their attorney and the bank attorney; yes, that right—the bank has their own attorney.

The home inspection is paid by the buyer, usually at the time of inspection.

Title search is paid by the buyer.

Bank appraisal fee is paid by the buyer.

If a new survey is required, that is also paid by the buyer. Lots of times, both parties agree to split the cost for a new survey.

Transfer tax is paid by the seller. You really want to make sure the deed is transferred into the new buyer's name—you never know what could happen.

Same goes for the recording of the deed. Both the transfer tax and recording of the deed are monies well spent.

Once you get past the underwriting and due diligence step in the process, you are closer to moving. But wait, you're not there quite yet. In the next chapter, we will discuss when to call the movers.

"I'm going to be homeless!" my client would cry. *"You're not going to be homeless,"* is what I kept assuring my clients, every time we spoke, every time we saw each other. Again and again, she would cry, "I'm going to be homeless!" My clients aren't homeless, and neither will you be, as long as you know what to do.

Finally, there is a closing date in sight, and all it took was a couple of months. If you haven't already called to get a quote from a moving company, now is the time. I suggest contacting at least three companies. You may want to have a folder or binder that will hold all the quotes and other paperwork you will need. Let them know you have a tentative closing date.

Once you have a closing date, you can call the utility companies. Contact the water, gas, electric, and cable companies, and advise them of the move. Don't worry about what to say; they receive these calls all day long. Just tell them you will be selling your home and have a tentative closing date, and you want to stop or change the service. It's best to coordinate the transfer with the new owners; hopefully, you can save them a reconnection fee.

Along with the utility companies, there are other services you might have, such as oil delivery, newspaper, an alarm company, pool service, landscaping service, etc.

Don't forget to forward your mail. You can do this by going to the post office in person or online, whichever is easier for you. A great idea is to leave a large, self-addressed, pre-paid envelope for any mail that might accidently get delivered to your former residence. This way, the new homeowner can just send it off to your new residence after they have collected a couple of pieces, or you may want to acquire a P.O. Box until you get re-established.

Having a place to move to after the sale of your home is important. I remember the time when a closing date was unexpectedly moved up from Friday to Monday, and we found this out on Sunday, the day before the closing. That meant the sellers had to finish packing on Sunday, find a place to live, and close on Monday. Talk about stressful! Luckily, they had already started taking action to find a place to live and were able to call and get into the new apartment on Monday, signing everything online. WHEW! One obstacle down—now about the packing. The homeowners were smart and had started cleaning out items they did not intend on bringing with them to their new place. They packed at least 1 box a day, which took about 15 minutes a box; so, basically, they had 98% of their items packed up. They also labeled each and every box with a list of the contents, so if they did need something, it could be easily located—another obstacle down. But what about the movers? Could the movers get there on a day's notice? Yes, they could. Sunday and Monday were long stressful days; however, it could have been so much more stressful if they had left the packing to the last minute, not gone to secure an apartment, not had a great moving company already lined up, and had not already contacted the utility companies. So a little planning ahead can save you an enormous amount of stress and thousands of dollars.

In this case, they were moving from a condo into an apartment while waiting for their home to be completed; however, this might not be your case. You might be closing on the sale of one house and immediately closing on the purchase of your new home. Can you have both closings the same day? Absolutely. Having a professional, experienced team on your side is a huge benefit and can tackle any issues that arise. However, even with all the experienced professionals, you will want to have a plan B. As Lee Child has said, *"Hope for the best, plan for the worst."* No matter how much you plan, some things are just out of your hands.

It's usually not a good idea to move before the closing; sometimes deals may fall apart at the closing table. Having already vacated will put you in a precarious negotiating position—the buyers may feel they have an upper hand. Of course, always consult your attorney before making any decisions.

This means always having a backup plan: a family member or friend's house to go to. Hopefully, you won't need to take them up on their accommodations; however, it's better to have a plan and not need it than need it and not have it. Scout out some short-term rental apartments, just in case—you never know.

A great tip when moving into your new home is to label each room. Things can get hectic on moving day—movers asking what goes where—it takes five minutes of planning to save you hours of stress on the moving day. Label each room with a large piece of paper, written clearly with a marker, and attach the paper to the wall with painters tape; this way, when the sign is removed, the tape will not make any marks on the wall. Be sure to label each room: master bedroom; bedroom 1; bedroom 2; family room; etc. Remember, the movers have never been to your new house before, so they won't know which room is which. Also, label where the furniture will be placed in the room. This way, you can just say, "Oh, it goes in bedroom 3," and the movers will see the sign for bedroom 3, and another sign as to where to put the bed. Another great tip is to have 2 boxes with cleaning supplies. One box is the last box to leave the house you're moving from, and the other box is the first to arrive at the house you're moving to. In these boxes, have some supplies: soap, paper towels, toilet paper, light bulbs, and anything else you might need. You don't want to get to your new home and the kids need to use the restroom, but you can't find the toilet paper and soap.

There is just one more item to check off the list before the closing: the walk through, also known as the final inspection. This is when the buyers visit the home to ensure everything is the same as when they originally decided to purchase the home. Verify all the appliances are in working order, as well as the heat, A/C, electrical, hot water, etc., and that nothing was removed that should be there.

You did it. Congratulations, you made it to the closing table. The buyers are there, you're there, and the attorneys, the bank attorney, and a title representative are there. Some closings are somber (maybe there were more than the expected hiccups along the way), and others are very joyful. I truly wish the latter for you.

There's nothing like selling your home to a buyer who you know is going to have many happy times in the home you loved for so many years.

It's finally time to move on to the next chapter in your life.

Good luck,
Teri